THE TREE OGHAM

WRITTEN
AND
ILLUSTRATED
BY
GLENNIE KINDRED

THE TREE OGHAM.
© GLENNIE KINDRED
ALL RIGHTS RESERVED.

PUBLISHED BY: GLENNIE KINDRED.
3, DANBURY MOUNT. SHERWOOD. NOTTINGHAM. NG5 4BL.

PRINTED BY: 4 SHEETS DESIGN AND PRINT.
197, MANSFIELD RD. NOTTINGHAM. NG1 3FS.

DISTRIBUTED BY: COUNTER CULTURE.
BCM INSPIRE, LONDON. WC1N 3XX.
TEL/FAX: 01823 698895.

ISBN 0-9532227-2-1.

ALSO AVAILABLE FROM PUBLISHER OR DISTRIBUTOR

THE SACRED TREE BY GLENNIE KINDRED.
AN EXPLORATION OF 13 OF OUR NATIVE TREES. FOLKLORE, LEGENDS, TREELORE, HERBAL USES, USES OF THE WOOD, SPIRITUAL AND HEALING QUALITIES OF EACH TREE, AND COMMUNICATING WITH TREE SPIRITS.

THE EARTHS CYCLE OF CELEBRATION.
BY GLENNIE KINDRED.
A GUIDE TO THE EIGHT CELTIC FESTIVALS AND WAYS TO CELEBRATE THEM TODAY.
(GERMAN AND JAPANESE TRANSLATIONS AVAILABLE)

ALSO PRINTS AND CARDS OF SOME ILLUSTRATIONS

CONTENTS

The Tree Ogham 4
Celtic World View 6
Communicating with Trees 7
Making Your Ogham Sticks 9
The Trees ....
    1. Birch 10
    2. Rowan 13
    3. Alder 16
    4. Willow 18
    5. Ash 21
    6. Hawthorn 24
    7. Oak 26
    8. Holly 28
    9. Hazel 30
    10. Apple 33
    11. Vine 36
    12. Ivy 38
    13. Broom 40
    14. Blackthorn 42
    15. Elder 44
    16. Fir 47
    17. Gorse 49
    18. Heather 51
    19. Aspen 53
    20. Yew 55
Using Your Ogham Sticks for Divination 58

4.

THE TREE OGHAM
ITS EVOLUTION AND CONTINUATION

The origins of the Tree Ogham (pronounced OH-AM) lie with the Celtic tribes who migrated to Britain from the Continent around 700 - 500 BC. There is no evidence of any Ogham script found on the Continent, but there are 320 inscribed standing stones surviving in the British Isles today, mostly in S. Ireland and Wales. There is even recent evidence of the Ogham script being used in N. America, opening up new evidence of Celtic migration.

      The inscribed Ogham stones were all carved about 300 - 700 AD. There aren't any inscriptions later than this, although the knowledge of the Ogham system was passed down orally until it was recorded in some medieval manuscripts — The Book of Leinster in the twelfth century; The Book of Ballymote in 1391, and the Book of Lecan in 1416. These manuscripts concern themselves with recording how the Ogham was used as an alphabet system, but the descriptions of each letter and its related tree are full of poetic reference and could hold many clues to their deeper meanings.

      There have been many suggestions as to what the Ogham was used for in its time. The Book of Ballymote reveals how it was used as a secret sign language, using the shinbone as the central stemline, and the fingers crossing it making the letters. Certainly the Ogham allows the practitioner to memorize and store data which enhances further understanding of abstract concepts in a language of encoded symbolism.

I have kept the original order of the Tree Ogham as recorded in the Book of Ballymote and have found a very clear pattern of spiritual understanding unfolds as each tree's subtle energy is understood. I suggest you make an Ogham stick for each tree which can be used in a similar way to the runes. The complete list of the Tree Ogham is found on the back cover. I make no claims that my interpretations are authentic to the Celtic tribes, only that they are relevant to today, and to those who are interested in spiritual and personal development, healing and trees.

It is a system which encourages you to spend time with trees. Sadly our trees are mostly ignored today, where once they were venerated for their many gifts, which were the mainstay of people's lifestyles. I have a very strong feeling that they want our communication & involvement.

Their supreme gift, the air we breathe, needs the greatest recognition of all. We have come a long way from the Celtic tribal understanding that everything is interconnected, and all of life is in delicate balance. The earth is sick, the air is bad, the water is polluted, the trees are dying, and yet the industrial and chemical madness runs on barely checked.

We are part of a new tribe, the Warriors of the Rainbow, as foretold by the Hopi prophecy. It is up to us to do all we can to save our earth, to save the trees, to ensure the good health of future generations.

Every single thing we do which is life-affirming, supports and aids the healing process. Together we can change the world.

CELTIC WORLD VIEW

This particular Tree Ogham has developed into a natural synthesis between what I understand of the Celtic Spiritual Tradition and the unfolding of a new spirituality emerging now as we enter the Aquarian Age.

I am inspired in my understanding of the Celtic world view by the intensely rhythmic interlinking patterns of their artwork which speaks to my unconscious mind more keenly than any words. The Celtic patterns communicate their awareness that every action has repercussions on many different levels of existence. There is an understanding that the physical, mental & spiritual aspects are intrinsically interlinked. There is also an acceptance of the inherent personal responsibility which this demands.

We know from legends and documented evidence that they were unafraid of death and believed in an afterlife and rebirth. Intrinsic to this was their belief in parallel universes, co-existing with our own 3-dimensional world governed by time (BITH).

The Celtic Otherworld can be reached through hidden doorways, stone circles, barrows, sacred groves, or through trance, meditation and altered states of mind. It can symbolically be thought of as above this one. A place of angels & spirit guides, loosened from the confines of earthly desires and time. The Underworld is very distant from this one, the Faerie Realms, slipping out of time. Harder to enter and even harder to get out of again.

COMMUNICATING WITH TREES

When we walk in the woods we generally feel a great sense of peace and oneness with nature. One of the reasons for this is that we have entered the interconnecting energy fields of the trees. We can feel their harmonious balanced flow of energy which is deeply healing and is part of our natural internal connection to Gaia.

We receive this balanced flow of energy whether we are conscious of it or not, but there are ways in which we can make a deeper conscious connection to a tree, which can aid emotional and spiritual healing.

If you are drawn towards a tree, this is the beginning of the communication already establishing itself. Make physical contact with the tree. Sitting with your back against its trunk is good. Give yourself and the tree time to tune into each other. Relax. Open your heart to the spirit of the tree and try not to prejudge what will happen. Visualize breathing the atmosphere of the tree into your heart chakra. Let your thoughts flow, and as with meditation, gently bring your focus back to the tree, each time you are aware of your thoughts wandering too far.

Learning to do a new skill takes time and practice. You will find your own ways which work for you. Always listen to your intuition and trust your innermost impressions.

When you have finished, always thank the tree, even if nothing appeared to happen.

It is important to spend time with the trees at different times of the year, different weather conditions and different times of the day, or night. This will bring you to a closer understanding of the trees and yourself.

Some times of the year are best for recognising different trees, eg catkins or flowers in the spring, or fruit in the autumn. Use these times to locate the trees in your area.

Further understanding will be gained by studying their folk lore and history, their place in the myths and legends and their role in the evolution of humankind.

Using the trees gifts of fruit, flowers, leaves and bark, enhances and deepens your personal relationship with the trees. It means that you spend more time with them, gathering and collecting their gifts to eat, or for making medicines. This builds up a relationship with them which is rich in involvement, communication and continuity.

It is good to keep a personal record of your communication with the trees, so that you can look back on it. Write the date each time, record your insights, how you felt at the time, what you learnt about yourself and the tree.

It is now understood that our emotions have a powerful affect on our health. Negative emotions, over a long period, will cause ill health, and positive emotions keep the life energy strong and will contribute significantly to the healing process.

Throughout the book I have recommended taking the Bach Flower Remedies, (or any other make of flower essence) where they are relevant. They will not suppress negative attitudes but will transform them into the positive side of that particular energy, stimulating one's own potential for self-healing. Sitting with a particular tree on a daily basis would provide the vibrational shift on the emotional level, but this is not always possible. Taking the flower essence of that tree is a realistic alternative.

MAKING OGHAM STICKS

Make each stick as you make contact with each tree. If you find a recently cut branch that you can cut your stick from, that is good, but do not use old wood that is lying around under the tree. It is important that the stick has the vibrational essence of the tree contained within it, and so it is better to ask the tree for a stick. Truly listen to the tree's response. If you feel a strong sense of no, you won't be able to cut, but be patient, you might be led to where there is recently cut wood, or try another tree on another day.

Remember always to thank the tree and to treat the tree with love and respect. This attitude has a clear positive effect on both the trees and ourselves, and helps to build a bond of friendship.

With the secateurs, cut a straight piece of wood about 1cm diameter and 8-10 cms long. It will shrink considerably, and there are 20 of them in total, so better to keep them small. The bark is best stripped off immediately before it shrinks onto the wood, but you might decide not to take it off at all, or to just take off some of it. Leave your stick outside for a week or so to dry out. Then shape it, carve it, sand it, whatever you decide to do. The Ogham symbol may be carved on, inked or painted.

All the time you are working, establish a conscious link between your stick and the tree. Focus on what you know about this tree on every level you can think of. This helps you to build up your knowledge on different levels of understanding. You will see how these overlap. Store your sticks in a bag made of a natural material.

Any twiggy bits left over can be put in water and appreciated, or you might try planting 9 cm sticks in compost (remove leaves) to grow into new trees.

BIRCH
B · BEITHE

NEW START
NEW BEGINNINGS
INCEPTION
BIRTH
REBIRTH
SPRING TIME · FERTILITY ·
NEW IDEAS · NEW OPPORTUNITIES ·
A JOURNEY
AN INITIATION
A CLEANSER – DRIVING OUT EVIL
TO NOURISH
CONNECTIONS TO THE YOUNG
CHANGE – LEAVING BEHIND OLD PATTERNS, WAYS, THINGS OR PEOPLE WHOSE INFLUENCE IS DETRIMENTAL TO YOU.
LOSS OF FAMILIAR THINGS.
LOSING FEAR OF UNKNOWN
WELCOMING CHANGES
GOOD FORTUNE AND HAPPINESS
ENERGIZING AND VITALIZING
PROTECTING

UNDERLYING ENERGY

THE BIRCH IS THE FIRST OF THE TREES IN THE OGHAM AND IS THE BEGINNING OF YOUR OWN PERSONAL JOURNEY THROUGH THE TREES. EACH TREE WILL GIVE YOU NEW INSIGHTS AND HEALING AS YOUR JOURNEY UNFOLDS.

THE BIRCH IS THE FIRST TREE TO COLONIZE NEW GROUND, DROPPING ITS leaves and twigs to enrich the soil for other trees to follow. It is thus a tree of great life-giving properties, vitality and nourishment.

The Birch always means a new beginning, a new opportunity, a new journey, physical or spiritual. It is a time to prepare yourself for changes. To begin any new situation, it helps to consciously put yourself in a different frame of mind. You might need to spiritually prepare yourself, leaving behind old patterns, ways of thinking, or hopes. The Birch has always been used in the past as a cleanser and for driving out evil. Now is the time to consciously rid yourself of any unhelpful influences in your life, which can hold you back and stop you moving forwards. Shed the old unhelpful aspects of your life, as the Birch sheds its bark. This will make way for the new to come in.

Whatever you must do, do it now, state your intent, clear the way, cleanse your aura (visualize it sparkling bright), cleanse your room (wash everything with salt water), cleanse your crystals (bury them in salt, wash them, leave them in moonlight to recharge). Find your own ways to clean out, clear out and prepare for a new start. Welcome change. Feel the strength & vitality which you will need and which is yours.

You may find you experience difficulty with dealing with change, and the loss of familiar things, but one of the lessons of Birch energy is to learn to trust that all will be well, and not to fear the unknown.

Nourish yourself and those around you, while preparing for changes, and the love you put out will ensure you are on the right path.

COMMUNICATING WITH BIRCH

The first thing to do is to go and find a birch tree which you can visit with ease. Return to the tree whenever possible. Get to know the tree and its surroundings and sit with your back against its trunk sensing its own special vibration.

It may take a while to find a silver birch you can sit with undisturbed, but keep looking out for their white trunks and you will find one you are drawn towards.

There are many different ways of being with, and communicating with trees. I have outlined some of the ways which I find harmonious in the section 'Communicating with Trees' but it is always important to follow your own intuitive responses and what feels good to you.

Make your intentions known to the tree and that you wish to make an ogham stick with the intention of communicating with birch energy. In time you will feel drawn towards a twig on the tree which has been offered to you by the tree. Refer to the section on making ogham sticks for details of this process. Always remember to thank the tree for its gift.

When communicating with the birch, take your ogham stick, establishing a link between the stick, the tree and yourself. Use whatever ritual or intuitive means of communication feels right to you or simply 'be' with the tree, open-hearted and receptive to receiving it's wisdom and healing vibration. When you are ready to break contact, do so slowly, always thanking the tree. Keep a record of your feelings and communication with the trees.

ROWAN
L · LUIS

PROTECTION FROM HARMFUL INFLUENCES
INTUITION AND INSIGHTS
INCREASED PSYCHIC POWERS
VISIONS · PORTENTS OF FUTURE EVENTS
DIVINATION
MEDITATION
VITALITY AND SPIRITUAL STRENGTH
TENACITY · REFUSAL TO GIVE UP

UNDERLYING ENERGY

THE INFLUENTIAL ENERGY OF ROWAN PROVIDES PROTECTIVE HELP AND AN INCREASE IN PSYCHIC ABILITIES, TO AID THE POTENTIAL SET IN MOTION BY THE BIRCH.

ROWAN TWIGS HAVE BEEN USED THROUGHOUT THE AGES AS A PROTECTION AGAINST EVIL, ENCHANTMENTS, BAD LUCK, AND ANY UNHELPFUL INFLUENCES. IT CAN INCREASE YOUR ABILITY TO RECEIVE FOREWARNINGS OR foreknowledge of previously unknown outside influences which may be affecting you. It strengthens your personal power so that you can withstand any psychic attack, be it intentional or unintentional.

The Rowan is connected to the Celtic festival of Imbolc which is associated with the Goddess Bridget who kindles the divine fire of inspiration and visions, and represents the rebirth of the spirit.

It is good to start meditating every day if you don't already, even if you begin by only doing it for 10 minutes. As the days go on you will find you will be able to slip into it for longer. It will free the mind of its surface clamour and leave openings for the clarity of divinely inspired thought.

It is a good time for inspired poetry and drawing, candle-gazing, scrying and any form of divination.

Ask for guidance and help from your guides and helpers. They can only help if you ask. Learn to read the messages and communications that the spirit realms leave you in everyday occurences.

Developing your psychic powers and trusting your own insights & intuition generates in return, a quickening of personal power and spiritual understanding.

COMMUNICATING WITH ROWAN

As with the Birch, find a Rowan tree which you can visit easily and make contact with it in ways which are comfortable to you. Make yourself your second ogham stick, and take it with you when communicating with the Rowan. Open yourself to receiving the healing powers the Rowan has to give. It is good to record the impressions you receive from the trees so you don't forget the flashes of inspired thought you have.

Rowan wood has been used magically throughout the centuries for protection and warding off evil. If you feel you need its protective influence, wear a sprig in your hat, or make yourself a small talisman from the wood to wear round your neck. You can also carry some berries and bark in a small healing pouch which you can carry or wear. It is a good wood for carving if you wish to work further with these properties.

Rowan wands have been a favoured magical tool and can be handled and used whenever the Rowan's influence is needed. Some people do not like the idea of cutting living wood, but if you ask the tree, explaining what you want it for, and truly experience the tree's reply, you will find that most trees willingly give their wood. The living wood holds more of the vital energy of the tree which makes the wand more effective, and of course is strongest. You will need to decide what size you would like to make your wand. Walking sticks of rowan are for those who wish to do night walking. You might want to strip all the bark off, or only some of it, decorate it, or carve it. It is good to be aware while you are doing it that you are creating a sacred tool, and keep awareness of what its uses are, so that understanding of the Rowan's qualities may grow.

3 ALDER
F· FEARN

FIRE AND WATER
ACTIVE AND RECEPTIVE
BALANCE
PRESERVATION
A SHIELD
PROTECTION
CHALLENGES
DISCRIMINATION
FOUNDATION
SPIRITUAL WARRIOR
INNER CONFIDENCE

UNDERLYING ENERGY

THE ALDER, LIKE THE ROWAN, HAS PROTECTIVE QUALITIES, BUT IT IS MORE THE PROTECTION A SPIRITUAL WARRIOR MIGHT NEED IN GOING BOLDLY FORTH INTO THE UNKNOWN.

THE ALDER ENERGY WILL HELP YOU TAKE UP CHALLENGES, MOVE INTO NEW SITUATIONS AND FACE THINGS WHICH YOU HAVE PREVIOUSLY AVOIDED. IT IS A BALANCED ENERGY ASSOCIATED WITH FIRE ON THE ONE HAND, WHICH WILL BRING A MASCULINE DIRECT APPROACH, AND YET ITS ELEMENT IS WATER, FEMININE AND RECEPTIVE. IN THE PAST THE WOOD WAS MOSTLY USED FOR ITS UNIQUE PROPERTIES OF BECOMING STRONGER WHEN IMMERSED IN WATER. IN CELTIC LORE, SPIRIT IS REPRESENTED BY WATER.

IT IS ALSO IMPORTANT FOR US TO BE AWARE OF WHAT IS GOING ON BELOW THE SURFACE AS WELL AS

On the physical level, the Alder could be a catalyst for changes and challenges in your life. This will ultimately bring you healing and a deeper understanding of yourself, even though these experiences might be difficult at the time. The Alder will help you to balance your fire and water qualities. To know when to move forwards, with strength and courage, challenging everything which doesn't ring true, and when to find inner stillness, and receptivity to divine inspiration which will guide your actions, are the lessons of Alder. They will provide a firm foundation for your life as a spiritual warrior.

Communicating with Alder

You will find the Alder along the river banks. It is particularly easy to spot in the spring when it is surrounded by a red haze formed by its reddish brown catkins.

It has always been a protected tree, associated with the Sidhe (the Faerie Realms or Underworld in Celtic lore)

Once you find one, there are usually several, so you will have to intuitively see which one is more welcoming and open to communication with you. With due ceremony and thanks to the tree make yourself your third Ogham stick. Write down any thoughts or experiences you have with the trees, it will be a wonderful record of your journey.

You might like to make yourself a shield out of Alder twigs, its design and decoration a fancy of your own. It is not a natural weaving material so be prepared for a challenge. As you weave, open yourself to understanding the protective qualities of the Alder.

4 WILLOW
S. SAILLE

THE UNCONSCIOUS
EXPRESSED EMOTIONS
INTUITION
FEMALE
THE MOON
FERTILITY
DREAMS
INSPIRATION
VISIONS
SEERSHIP

UNDERLYING ENERGY

The essential energy of the Willow is the power to go forth, into the unknown, with greater confidence and trust in ourselves and our abilities. It greatly enhances the power of the intuition, inspired leaps of the imagination, and makes connections to our unconscious and deeply buried emotions.

Willow will allow the emotions to come through to the surface. Deep emotional pain blocks the energy of the body and

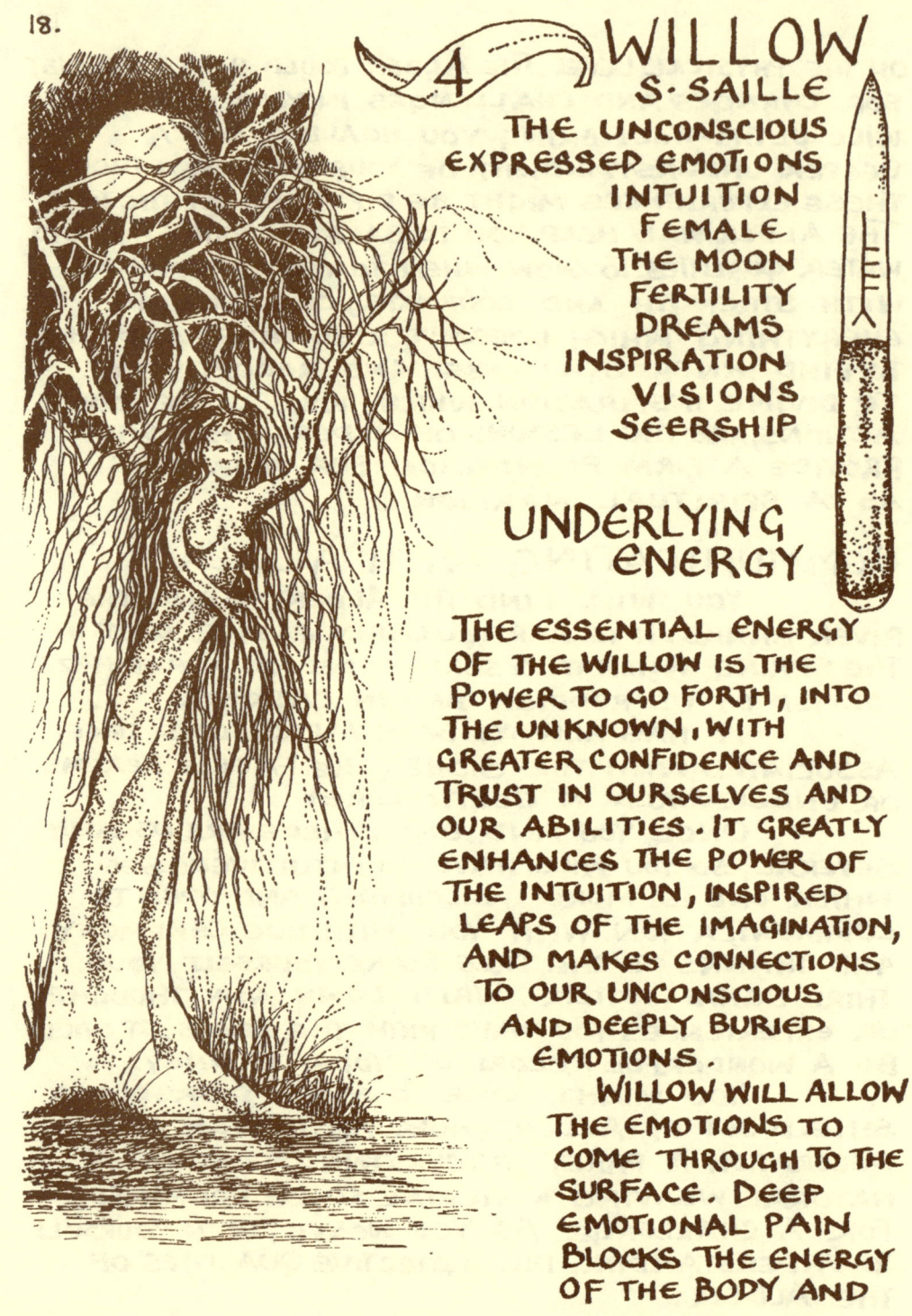

can cause many illnesses. Willow will encourage you to move through the many levels of sadness, express the pain through tears and grief, and by moving through the emotions, facilitate healing. When one of the Willow's twigs become disconnected it can easily grow into a new tree, teaching us that contained in a loss or a separation, is always new life, a new direction, and the capacity for growth and healing. The Willow Bach Flower remedy can be used to enhance this process.

The Willow's watery energy encourages flowing, letting go and surrendering to the emotions. Perhaps we all need to break the ethos of our culture and give in more readily to how we feel, finding ways to express ourselves. It is possible through life's experiences to become stuck in certain emotional patterns. Any negative state can be changed with the help of the Willow energy, which encourages emotional movement. Rather than resist what we are feeling, we can let go of conditioned responses and find new ways of dealing with emotional situations.

The Willow particularly stimulates our ability to follow our intuition, and find our own meanings behind what lies on the surface. We have been taught to regard our intuition as unreliable, but this just isn't true, and we must use it more in order to develop it.

Willow is recommended for use when seeking to understand ancient ways or another's spiritual teachings. It will help you assimilate different levels of information, and move quickly through your emotional responses to appreciate and see the patterns behind the information. Once the information has been assimilated, it can be utilized for change in your life.

COMMUNICATING WITH WILLOW

Willow is easy to recognise and is found growing along river banks. Sometimes it is found growing right out into the river which provides an unusual place to sit. Listen to your intuition especially when communicating with the willow, and write down any thoughts, poems, insights and feelings you have while you are there.

The willow will enhance visions and seership and you might like to make yourself a wand for this purpose as well as your Ogham stick. If you want to increase your dream life, or feel you have lost touch with your dreams, sleep with a willow wand or your willow Ogham stick under your pillow. You will soon find your dreams becoming more accessible. Write them down upon waking, and open your intuition to interpreting them. This can lead to healing emotional problems and releasing tensions in your life.

The willow is a very receptive tree, used to contact with humankind through the ancient tradition of basket making. Its pliant twigs make it easy to weave, and learning how to make baskets will ensure you have plenty of contact with this tree and its beneficial properties.

5 ASH
N·NION

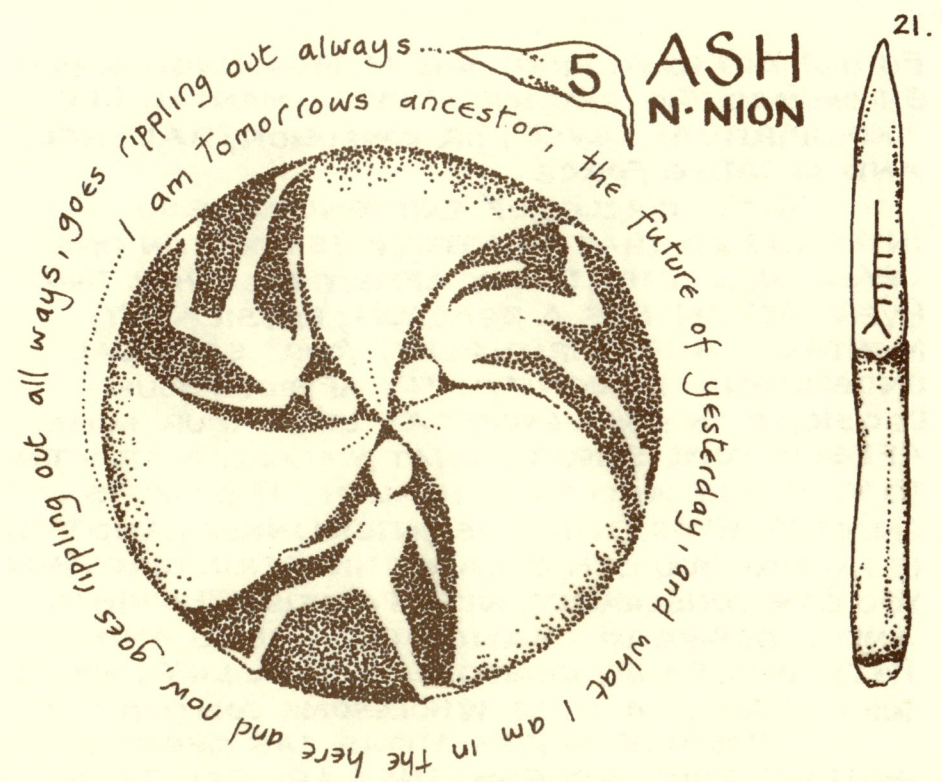

I am tomorrows ancestor, the future of yesterday, and what I am in the here and now, goes rippling out all ways, goes rippling out always...

A KEY TO A UNIVERSAL TRUTH
EVERY ACTION HAS A REACTION
INTERLINKING CIRCLES OF EXISTENCE
HEALING THE INNER CHILD
THE POWER OF POSITIVE AFFIRMATIONS.

UNDERLYING ENERGY

The Ash holds a key to a universal truth, the understanding of which is essential to the spiritual warrior. Your actions, and thoughts form part of an endless chain of events. Whatever you do in the physical world affects other levels of your existence and being. The Celts called these 3 circles of existence Abred, Gwynedd, and Ceugant, which can be translated as past, present and future but have much wider meanings which encompass the physical level, mental level and spiritual level; or confusion, balance and creative force.

The 3 circles of existence are so interlocked that whatever is done on one level will inevitably affect the other two. Every action has a reaction; physically, mentally and spiritually. Your spiritual understanding constantly affects your decisions in your everyday life. Your mind affects your spirit, what you are attracting to yourself and your health. The list is endless. Everything is interlinked, and there is no way you can escape this structure. But you can consciously, with positive thoughts and a desire to change old habits and patterns, bring changes in your life; which will lead to a more wholesome continuum.

Positive affirmations can greatly enhance this process. They are repetitive positive mantras used as an aid to healing the inner child, healing associated illnesses, and breaking the negative patterns which might have been built up over the years which are causing damage. I highly recommend 'You Can Heal Your Life' by Louise Hay, but there are many other excellent books on this subject.

Communicating with Ash

The Ash was considered by the Druids to be one of their 5 sacred trees. It is not hard to find as it has a lot of distinctive features. Sit with your back to its trunk and breathe in the wisdom of this tree. As before, ask for a twig with which to make your Ogham stick, truly feeling the tree's response, and thanking the tree for its healing and its gift.

Now you have 5 ogham sticks, and it is really important the more you get, that you keep on working with all of them, and the trees. This means you will internalize their meanings and understand the way they interconnect and follow on from each other. Lay them out in their correct ogham order, and also in different orders and combinations, and go over what you know about them. Lay them with their symbols on the underside, so that you learn to recognise the wood and its bark.

You might like to make a spear out of ash, to remind you of your responsibilities as a spiritual warrior. Go about this in a spiritual frame of mind, while you are cutting the wood, shaping it and decorating it.

A guided visualization or otherworld journey will connect you to a circle of existence which is beyond the physical. Make yourself comfortable, perhaps holding your spear, and imagine yourself taking a walk in the woods. At this stage it would be good to visualize the 5 trees you have met so far. How do you relate to the different trees on your journey? Which trees are more plentiful? Do you sit with any? Do any birds animals or people appear?

Leave your otherworld forest when you are ready, surfacing slowly and thanking your guides and the trees for their help. Write down the date and any impressions, and use your intuition to interpret what you saw and felt on the journey.

HAWTHORN H HUATH

LOVE
THE HEART
CLEANSING
RELEASING BLOCKED ENERGY
PROTECTION
PREPARATION FOR SPIRITUAL GROWTH

UNDERLYING ENERGY

The Hawthorn has the ability on the subtle level to open the heart to spiritual growth and love. It continues and aids the process begun with the Ash of healing the inner child and resolving with love any areas where you might be manifesting a victim complex that will keep you vulnerable and lacking in power and energy.

The Hawthorn will release blocked energy, not only relieving stress but creating an ability to trust and let go of fear. As fear is released, great psychic energy is liberated, primarily in the heart centre. Blocked energy in the aura becomes dislodged and the way for the energy of love is opened.

I believe the Hawthorn is very much involved in humankind's evolution into the Aquarian Age of a more open-hearted humanitarian attitude to life, love and spirituality. I sense a willingness in the Hawthorn energy to help us and be part of this transformation.

COMMUNICATING WITH HAWTHORN

This is a wild and enchanted tree under the protection of the faerie realms and the old magic, and as such it should be greatly respected.

Look for an old tree if possible, and keep your eyes open for cut wood along the hedgerows, as it is constantly cut back by the farmers.

A talisman made of Hawthorn will enhance your ability to release love, open your heart and align yourself to your spiritual development. Healing wands can be given as a token of friendship and love.

OAK
D·DUIR

INNER STRENGTH
ENDURANCE
COURAGE
A DOORWAY
SELF-DETERMINATION

UNDERLYING ENERGY

The Oak is a doorway to inner spirituality. It is the strength which is unfolding before you with each new connection along the Ogham tree journey. Now you have the inner power to overcome and survive any situation.

The Oak will lead the way to the truth, especially about past layers of action, and this revelation brings strength and vision, and a gateway to new understanding.

Oak restores the will and self-determination that may have become weakened in times of stress, and restores faith in the vision of what you are working towards. Use of the Bach Flower Remedy will also help, but go to the Oak tree itself when you need to find the courage and strength to fight against great difficulties.

There is a warning though about stubborn strength which resists and breaks in the storm. Sometimes there is a need to rest, beneath an oak tree when possible, and use the accumulated wisdom and strength gained, to restore equilibrium. The strength of love has brought you this far, and this is the power which will endure.

COMMUNICATING WITH OAK

The Oak was sacred to the Druids who met beneath its mighty form, and planted it in groves to mark sacred places. It can reach a great age, often splitting open and providing unusual places to sit and communicate with its ancient wisdom. You might find a twig with which to make your Ogham stick, from a branch broken off in a storm.

An oak wood is a good place to walk to fully absorb the truth behind the strength of the oak.

An oak wand would be ideal to make if you need to get in touch with your inner strength and power. Make it out of any piece of oak which suggests this use, and decorate it with anything which has power and meaning to you, such as beads, a stone with a hole in it, a special feather, coloured wools. While you are making it, feel the power and inner strength which is yours and will forever be a part of you.

HOLLY
T·TINNE

UNIFYING STRENGTH

RESTORED BALANCE

RESTORED DIRECTION

COMMUNICATION

UNCONDITIONAL LOVE

RESPONSIBILITY

UNDERLYING ENERGY

The evergreen Holly is a masculine tree and a powerful symbol of potent life energy. It will help restore direction in your life, uniting past actions with present actions, and past lives with your present life. It has the ability to unite two sides of a question or problem and help you find a balanced solution. It will provide you with the raw energy to deal with draining emotional entanglements.

Bach wrote 'Holly protects us from anything which is not unconditional love. Holly opens the heart and unites us with divine love.' The Bach flower remedy Holly is to help those who are troubled by suspicion, hatred, jealousy, and revenge. All of these negative emotions greatly weaken your life force by causing constant inner turmoil and negative thought patterns. Holly will help you communicate more easily, bringing the inner turmoil out into the open so that it can be resolved.

Holly brings love and compassion, helping you understand your own pain as well as the pain of others. It facilitates the power of directed thought. Use this to psychically cut the emotional ties which have been formed by a draining relationship. Visualize them cut and dissolving away.

Holly will bring you great balanced power which will guide your actions towards unconditional love and compassion, and an increased detachment from emotional turmoil.

Communicating with Holly

Holly is a tree of protection, and was a protected tree, considered unlucky to cut down. As such many old trees have survived in hedgerows and in cottage gardens.

It might be possible to make your 8th Ogham stick from a necessary garden pruning, but remember still to cut with respect and love for the living tree. It has a beautiful white wood which is good for carving if you wish to spend more time with the Holly energy.

Meditating with the Holly, linking to Holly energy through your Ogham stick, or any other form of daily meditation, will provide a valuable understanding of the power of unconditional love. It is not an easy state to achieve, nor easy to fully understand. The Holly Ogham provides you with the opportunity to explore our responsibility to its potential.

HAZEL
C · COLL

9

DIVINATION
VISIONS
DEEP LISTENING
INTUITION
DIVINE SOURCE
ESSENCE
OF KNOWLEDGE
ESSENCE
OF BEING
WISDOM
CREATIVITY
TRANSFORMATION
CATALYST
THE FLOW

UNDERLYING ENERGY

HAZEL HAS THE ABILITY TO CONNECT CONSCIOUS MIND WITH THE UNCONSCIOUS MIND, BRINGING IDEAS TO THE SURFACE AND FACILITATING TRANSFORMATION OF DREAMS AND VISIONS INTO REALITY.

IT IS STRONGLY ASSOCIATED WITH MEDITATION AND A CONNECTION TO THE DIVINE SOURCE AND ESSENCE OF OUR BEING. IT BRINGS WISDOM AND KNOWLEDGE, AND AN INCREASE IN PSYCHIC ABILITIES, INTUITION AND INSPIRATION.

THERE IS A NEED TO HARNESS THESE QUALITIES, AND CHANNEL THEM INTO CREATIVITY. THE VISIONS WE ACT UPON NOW WILL CHANGE OUR FUTURE AND TRANSFORM OUR PRESENT. OUR DREAMS CAN BECOME OUR REALITY THROUGH CREATIVE, LIFE-ENHANCING SOLUTIONS IN AREAS OF OUR LIVES WHICH WE INTUITIVELY FEEL NEED CHANGING.

It is a good time to study and discover the teachings of any wise person, spiritual teacher or guru. Perhaps you will yourself become a teacher for another.

Hazel will bring healing through intuitively understanding the source or essence of any situation, and in acting upon the insights and inspirations gained. Let your intuition guide you, no matter how your rational mind might reject the ideas which have come to you. We have been brought up in a world where rational thought is honoured, but the intuition is not. It is time to redress the balance and give credibility to the intuitive process.

Let your creativity flow. Go with the flow of inspired thoughts. Approach all areas of your life and relationships with a heart which is open to inspired solutions. Follow an intuitive path rather than any well-thought-out plan.

Now is the time to change your daily routines, or your lifestyle. Everything you do, the food you eat, your job, your home, how you relate to others etc, is a reflection of what is at the core of your being and can show us much about ourselves.

Communicating with Hazel.

It is easier to spot the Hazel in the spring when the yellow catkins hang brightly against all the bare winter trees. It makes it easier to find them again later in the year when they are surrounded by a sea of green leaves.

The Hazel is a very easy tree to communicate with, and has been used to man coppicing its many trunks for his use.

As well as your 9th Ogham stick you might like to make yourself a walking stick or staff from one of its long straight stems. These make fine companions for a walk which will enhance any other communications from non-verbal beings such as other members of the plant kingdom, minerals and stones, or animals.

Make yourself a dowsing rod from a forked piece of hazel, and gripping a fork in each hand, pull them apart until you feel the pressure 'bite'. Focus your intent to look for underground water, and you will feel, and see, the stick bend back and twitch as you pass over the water.

In Irish folk lore and legend, it is the hazel nuts themselves which contain all wisdom, so it is a good idea to collect and eat them when they are in season.

Go to the hazel, and use your Ogham stick whenever your purpose is to gain knowledge and insights.

Lighting a fire, or candle, staring into the flames and letting the mind wander will aid communication with your guides and helpers. So will meditation. Both will allow your unconscious space to surface into the conscious mind.

Go to the hazel whenever you need to overcome any creative blocks, and whenever you wish for creative solutions to transform any situation from the mediocre to the truly inspirational.

10 APPLE
Q · QUEIRT

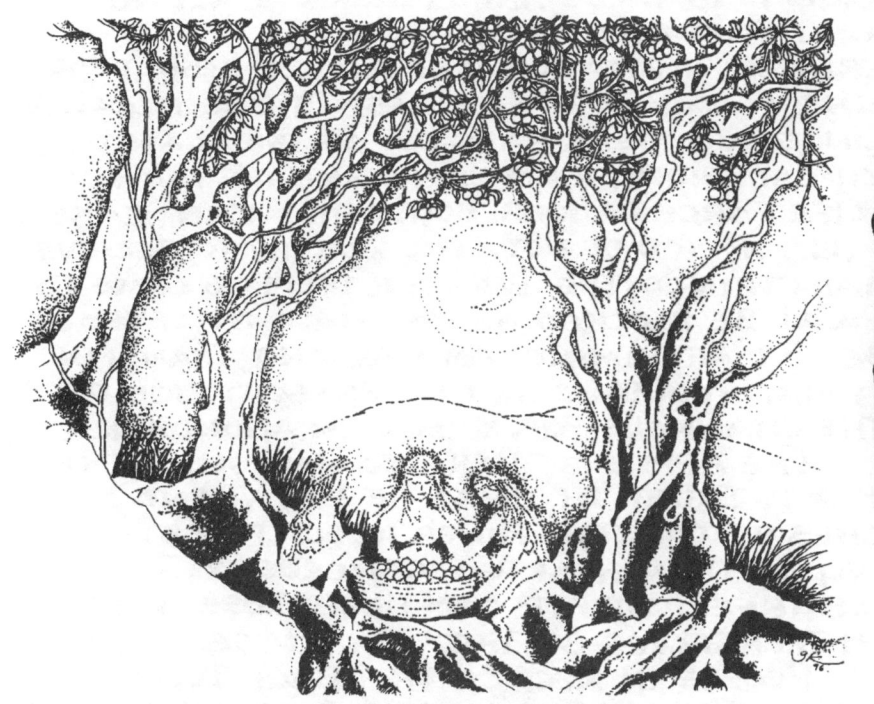

ABUNDANCE
OPEN HEARTED GENEROSITY
CLEANSING
GRATITUDE

UNDERLYING ENERGY

THE SHEER EXTRAVAGANT ABUNDANCE OF AN APPLE TREE IN AUTUMN IS THE KEY TO UNDERSTANDING WHAT THE APPLE HAS TO TEACH US. IT SHOWS US HOW TO GIVE ALL, IN TOTAL TRUST THAT ALL WILL BE REPLENISHED. IT TEACHES US TO OPEN OUR HEARTS TO THE ABUNDANCE IN OUR LIVES.

WHEN WE, LIKE THE APPLE TREE, GIVE ALL OF OURSELVES FREELY AND OPENLY, OUR hearts are open to receiving more. Holding back is a symptom of greed and insecurity. The Apple's message is to value and celebrate all you have in your life. Many feelings of bitterness, irritation and anger result from feeling a lack of worthiness. These negative feelings create a pattern of imbalance which can significantly reduce the flow of the life force in your body. This can make you ill. If you do not feel worthy to receive certain things, the way for them to come to you will be blocked as you have believed it to be. By affirming and feeling thankful for what you have in the present, you open up the channels for your own abundance.

The Apple is there to help all of us keep our trust in times of lack, and teaches us our true power is built up by giving, in open-hearted generosity. The Apple Tree's spirit can help those who harm themselves by their own miserliness.

People in need of the Bach Flower Remedy, Crab Apple, have a poor self-image, feel they are unclean, or in need of cleansing. They are more sensitive than most, taking in much more on the subtle levels. They can be over-anxious about dirt and fearful of contamination. They can sometimes attract entities which can attach themselves to people whose life force power is weak. The Apple remedy is a powerful cleanser, which can be used internally as well as externally. It will encourage acceptance of oneself and other peoples imperfections and restore a sense of beauty and love.

The Apple has close links to Otherworld journeying and the Celtic festival Samhain.

COMMUNICATING WITH APPLE

An Apple orchard would give you the best concentrated experience of Apple energy. Crab Apple trees have a wilder energy, and garden Apple trees a more friendly energy as they are used to human company.

It might be possible to make your 10th Ogham stick from a piece which needs pruning anyway, but still do so in a respectful frame of mind.

You might also like to make a wand out of Applewood, which could be used as an aid to Otherworld journeying. Its size and design is up to you, but something which fits comfortably in the hand is best.

Holding your wand, either sit beneath an Apple tree or imagine yourself sitting beneath an Apple tree, and imagine yourself looking out on a group of trees. Begin by thinking about the Apple tree and what you understand about its energy. Let your thoughts wander and see what comes into your mind. It is not a test! Relax! When you are ready, shift your attention to the other trees and see which ones are there, and what you understand about their energies. Go and sit with any you are drawn towards if you want. Do whatever you have a mind to do. Observe anything else of interest in this group of trees and when you are ready return to your starting point and surface slowly. See if you can interpret any messages from your spirit guides which may have been sent to you from this Otherworld. Write down what you think and the date.

VINE
M · MUIN

UNITING
TEACHING
INSPIRATION
DETERMINATION
INSTINCT
LOOSENS INHIBITIONS

UNDERLYING ENERGY

The interweaving of the vine provides the clue to its essential energy. It unites the other trees together as it grows from one to the other, linking the teachings of each into a whole concept.

Interlinking and weaving is part of understanding the patterns behind a learning process. Links are formed and parts of yourself become united. The vine has a determined energy which if used for teaching will help encourage and guide others without controlling them. It is a good lesson to learn. Not everybody has the same views as you, and respecting another's point of view is an important aspect of being a good teacher. It is better to inspire others than to force your views on them. This way each person finds their own path to follow. The Bach Flower Remedy Vine is used when someone has become domineering and over-rides the opinions and wishes of others.

The Vine brings an understanding of the different levels on which we interact, and awareness of the interweavings of the conscious and unconscious mind. The Vine will allow your perceptions to come to the surface, and it is up to you to trust them and act upon them when they do.

There is a danger of course that you might become lost in your own subjective intoxicating enthusiasm, but we have all been conditioned for so long to follow our logical intellectual mind that it is important to abandon yourself to another faculty. It is your conferred power and inherited right.

Communicating with Vine

The Vine is not strictly speaking a tree, but a climbing shrub, and is the only one of the Ogham which is not native. You might wish to substitute Bramble for Vine as it has many similarities.

If you find difficulty in getting the wood for your 11th Ogham stick, you could use wood which is not part of the Ogham such as Chestnut or Beech. This can be replaced when you find a piece of Vine. Lots of people grow vines in their conservatories, which are cut back every year, but the best wood is to be found from vines growing outside.

Try to imagine yourself as a vine, linking trees together. Link trees you have already studied, in groups of 2 or 3 or 4. Use your sticks to make bundles. Try to build up a picture of what these composite energies might be. Find combinations which fuse together well to make a complete picture.

Using a piece of Birch write out Ogham symbols on one stem from the bottom to the top, to make a message stick.

12 IVY
G·GORT

A WARNING
DETERMINED POWER
BINDING
RESTRICTING
SEARCH FOR THE SELF
ATTACHMENT
FREEDOM
UNITING

UNDERLYING ENERGY

There is a fierce, determined power to the Ivy. It has the ability to bind many trees together and restrict passage through the woods. It can eventually smother and kill a tree, even the mighty Oak. Should a dense Ivy thicket appear in one of your other world journeys, you should stop immediately and examine your motives, either there or in your life. This destructive aspect of the Ivy is a warning about wandering without thought and attention to the 'whys' and 'hows' of what you are doing.

The Ivy represents the search for the self, and the wandering of the soul in its desire for enlightenment. It will link you with others through the group collective soul.

It is up to you to understand whether your wanderings restrict and bind, or unite. Clinging to one tree, one concept, would be restricting and even damaging, but embracing many concepts and energy patterns will bring confidence and put you in touch with your own freedom and inner resources.

Freedom means going where you choose, but it is where you choose to go which will reveal your true inner perspective. It is what you choose to do with that freedom that will tell you much about what aspect of yourself still needs healing.

Communicating with Ivy

The Ivy is another of the Ogham Fews which is not a tree, but grows with the support of a host tree, like the Vine it will unite different trees together, although it can be much more destructive.

With support the Ivy can grow really thick trunks and with some searching it is possible to find a really old plant with which to commune and find the wood to make your 12th Ogham stick.

Meditate on directions you are taking and if these enhance or restrict your healing process.

BROOM
nG · nGETAL

CLEANING UP

SOUL OR ASTRAL TRAVEL

RESTORES HARMONY

UNDERLYING ENERGY

The first and obvious association with the broom is that of cleaning up or making a clean sweep. This can be done on the physical, mental, psychic and spiritual levels.

Physically clear out and clean your living space. Throw or give away any things which are no longer relevant to you, or which belong to your past and now hold you back by their associations

Creating harmony and light in your living space will greatly affect how you are when you are in it. You can cleanse the space by burning dried sage, but there are many other methods of clearing energy. Find out about them and see what works for you.

Sometimes it is the aura which needs cleaning. Entities can be attached to you without you knowing. They can be very draining and need to be cleared off. Smoking dope causes holes in your aura which take 7 years to heal, and cause constant psychic leaks which rob you of your vital energy.

You can cleanse the aura by burning dried sage and wafting the smoke around the outside of the body, but if you suspect you need a stronger clearing, cleaning or healing, it is probably a good idea to go and see a spiritual or psychic healer. She or he will be able to see or sense any areas which need attention, and will have the necessary skills to promote healing. Also they will be able to help you facilitate in this process — often by giving you visualization exercises, meditation exercises and affirmations.

Communicating with Broom.

The Broom is most often found in wild places. It is a sheltering plant offering protection from the wind. It is probably better to link with a group of plants, but that is up to you.

In order to get a piece of wood large enough to make your 13th Ogham stick, you will have to cut quite a large piece, so why not make yourself a brush with what is left. Bind the stalks together with string to make a handle.

The Broom is associated with astral or soul travel. The broom was the vehicle 'witches' used to travel on and would have been made out of broom. It has narcotic properties which ties in with this.

Use your Ogham stick and broom or brush to facilitate a journey on the astral plane. Either let yourself be drawn along, or specifically imagine yourself visiting a place of your choosing.

Ask your guides for help in showing which areas of your life need cleaning up.

14 BLACKTHORN
ST/Z STRAIPH

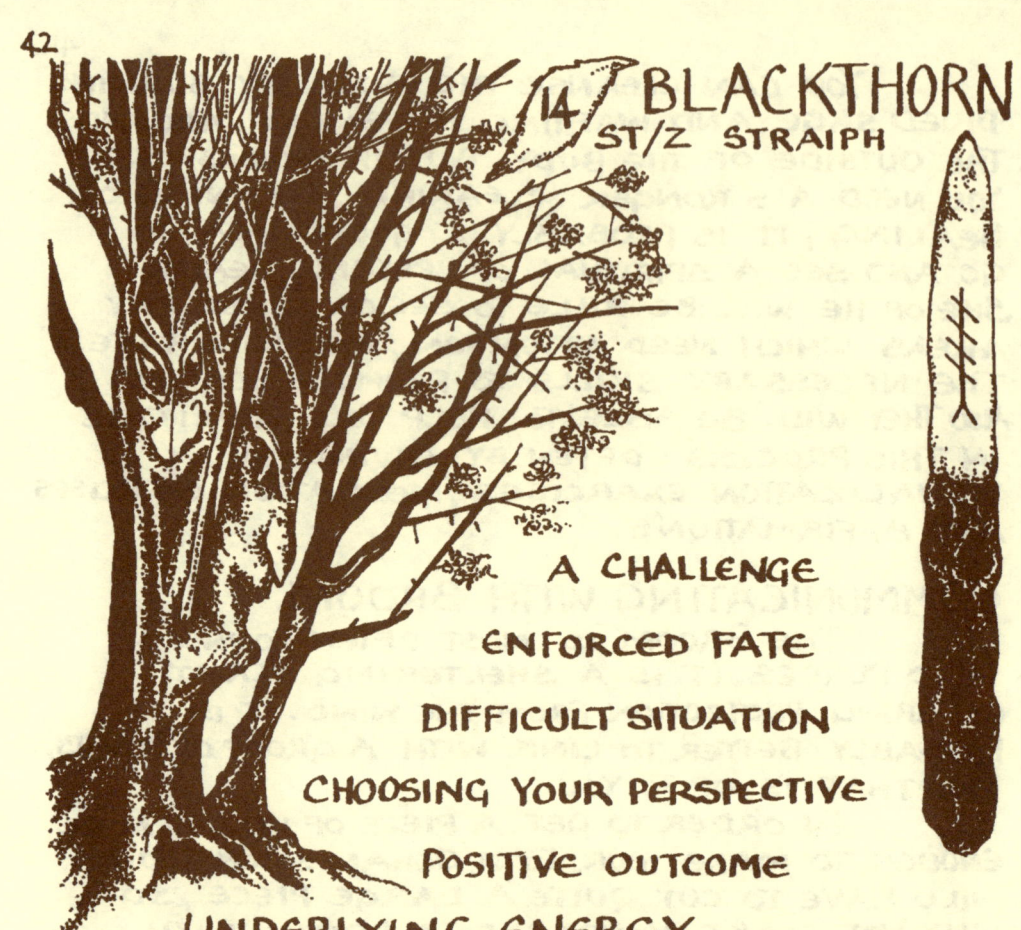

A CHALLENGE

ENFORCED FATE

DIFFICULT SITUATION

CHOOSING YOUR PERSPECTIVE

POSITIVE OUTCOME

UNDERLYING ENERGY

Blackthorn is a harsh energy which at first seems hostile, unpleasant and challenging. Sometimes events in your life seem to force you to take a path you do not readily wish to take. Fate seems to take over, unforeseen events happen and you feel you have no choice. You always do ofcourse. The choice lies in how you deal with these situations.

The lesson to be learnt from the blackthorn is to recognise when not to fight against fate, but to go along with it, looking for the positive outcome & where it is leading you. Try to recognise the new direction or opportunity as it unfolds from the chaos. If your perspective is positive then the outcome for you will inevitably be positive. The key is not striving against the situation but using your spiritual strength, knowledge and understanding to see beyond the negative. Every single thing that happens has positive repercussions, even if it is hard to see at the time.

Meditation will help to keep you in a more detached frame of mind. Be good to yourself, and find ways to nurture your spirit. Harsh times will pass, and lead to a new season of flowering.

Communicating with Blackthorn

It is not easy to enter into communication with blackthorn trees, because they are so thorny on all levels! I look upon the blackthorn as a grumpy old man - who has a heart of gold really.

You can't get close physically to a blackthorn, so sit a little distance away and open yourself to what the tree has to offer you. A challenging friendship, but one which will eventually show its benefits.

The wood is extremely hard, and be very wary of those thorns, they can cause septicaemia very easily. When looking for the right piece of wood for your 14th ogham stick listen to the trees guidance and thank it for its gift. It may help you find some wood which has already been cut. It quickly grows into impenetrable thickets, so farmers do have to keep it in check

ELDER
R·RUIS

**TRANSFORMATION
RENEWAL
REGENERATION
WISDOM OF AN ELDER**

UNDERLYING ENERGY

THE ELDER PROVIDES A NATURAL PROGRESSION FROM THE BLACKTHORN AND OFFERS HELP AND UNDERSTANDING TO DEAL WITH CHANGES. THE ELDER IS A TREE OF REGENERATION, growing easily from all parts. The tree has a wise old woman energy and has the protection of the old Crone aspect of the Celtic Triple Goddess. She guards the entrance to the Underworld and Death, the threshold of consciousness, and the dark inner mysteries. She gives us the wisdom to honour the beginning in every end, and the end in every beginning. Each death, each end will bring a new start, a rebirth.

The Elder provides the wisdom to deal with changes and to help you to see them as transformation & renewal. She reminds you of the never ending cycle of life, death and rebirth, bringing power and hope to a dark and difficult situation. She is a true Elder among the trees.

Understanding this process will lead to a mature and balanced outlook which will bring great inner strength and wisdom.

Sometimes there is a need to let go of things which are holding you back. Sometimes this will be forced upon you and Elder will help you understand that the endless cycles of change will stop you stagnating, and move you into new beginnings.

COMMUNICATING WITH ELDER

I have always found the Elder to be a very approachable tree, used to a long history of humankind using all its gifts of bark, leaves, flowers and fruit for medicines, jams, drinks etc.

The wood is yellow and has a soft pith running through its center. Treat the Elder with the greatest respect and she will reward you with her blessings and her gifts. Make yourself your 15th

Ogham stick. Truly listening to the tree and honouring what you feel.

The elder makes natural beads, because of the soft pith which is easy to poke out. The elder can be coppiced giving straight sticks and promoting new growth each time a stick is cut. Cut a length of elder in the autumn about 1½ cms width, cut these into bead lengths, strip off the bark and let them dry out. You can poke the pith out with a nail and then sand them up to a smooth finish. They are easy to make and beautiful to feel. Wear them as an allegiance to the elder and as a reminder of her particular wisdom.

Relearning the age old cures for common ailments will connect you to the trees you gather from, the earth's abundance and your own power. The elder in particular has a wealth of medicinal and culinary uses worth exploring.

Try growing some new trees from the pieces of elder you have left from when you cut a branch for your stick or beads. Trim off most of the leaves and any flowers, to encourage growth into the roots. Plant pieces of about 8 cms long in pots of compost, water in dry weather but do not leave them sitting in water. Keep them potted for 2 years before planting out.

16 FIR
A-AILM

**OBJECTIVITY
FAR-SEEING
INNER WISDOM**

UNDERLYING ENERGY

HERE IS A TREE WHICH CAN SEE OVER GREAT DISTANCES. IT WILL HELP US TO DEVELOP THE PERCEPTIONS AND INSIGHTS NECESSARY TO SEE BEYOND THE PRESENT. IT WILL ALSO HELP US TO SEE AND UNDERSTAND THINGS FROM ANOTHER'S POINT OF VIEW AND WILL AID ANY situation where far-sighted vision is needed.

Here, seeing into the future comes from your own wisdom rather than received information in a divinatory sense, and is an indication of an inner perception which is inherent.

The Fir is a strong energy, a sign of good health and vigour, and an elevated state of mind. From here great things can be done, far-sighted actions taken and new objective insights gained.

The Fir indicates strength and healing learnt from past experiences.

COMMUNICATING WITH FIR

The only Fir tree which would have been native at the time of the Tree Ogham's use would have been the Scots Pine.

If possible find a single tree in an elevated position. Make contact with the tree in your usual way and make your 16th Ogham stick.

This is the first tree of the last Aicme, which are all vowels. Place your Ogham stick next to each of the others in turn and perceive the picture they make together.

All of the vowels of the A-Aicme have an inner wisdom inherent in their potential.

17 GORSE
O·ONN

GATHERING IN

SYNTHESIS

HARVESTING

UNDERLYING ENERGY

The Gorse or Furze bush flowers almost continuously and provides rich rewards for the gathering bees. Honey is linked to wisdom in Celtic legend, as it is the result of a lot of hard work. The Gorse is the epitome of a good harvest in your life, linking fulfilment and fruitfulness in the inner and outer worlds. The work you have put into cultivating your spiritual path has now come to fruition and the time is right for you to realize a goal or direction you wish for.

You will be able to gather together all the different elements you need in order to attain your purpose. There could be a great gathering together of people, materials or information which can be harnessed. You may feel like a magpie gathering treasures from here and there. You work with wisdom and an inspired vision, faith and hope.

Gorse is a Bach Flower Remedy for those who have lost their faith and hope in life and need it restoring to them. They feel their harvest has only brought them despair and illness, from which they see no cure. It is extreme hopelessness and despair, but Gorse has the power to restore hope and an ability to see illness as a positive experience.

Gorse can also facilitate a period of active internal synthesis. Sitting back, gathering yourself together, to come to a higher understanding of where you are at. It is a time to give thanks for all the inner rewards which you are now harvesting. Being aware of them will help you see ways to use them in the future.

Be aware that your attention could be scattered by the very act of gathering information and material, and you might forget the purpose behind it all.

Communicating with Gorse

The Gorse is found on moorland or common land, choosing a place away from the trees where it can bask in the sun — what a good idea! Find a gap in the gorse, lay down and drink in their heady scent. You will not harm the gorse by cutting your 17th Ogham stick. It will quickly grow new shoots again. But still treat the plant with respect and thank it for its gift.

It may be that you will just need to let the gorse stick dry out and sand it smooth without stripping off the outer bark.

Use your Ogham stick to meditate on your harvest and what you would like to do with it now.

This is another vowel and can be combined with other Ogham sticks.

18. HEATHER
U - UR

AN OPEN GATEWAY
BETWEEN
SPIRIT AND MATTER

FOCUSED PASSION
HEALING
LIFTING THE SPIRIT
OUTGOING
CARING FOR OTHERS

UNDERLYING ENERGY

HEATHER IS ANOTHER PLANT WHICH IS ASSOCIATED WITH BEES, HONEY AND WISDOM. THE GATEWAY BETWEEN THE SPIRITUAL INNER WORLD AND THE OUTER WORLD IS OPEN AND HOW YOU GO ABOUT YOUR LIFE IS VERY MUCH A REFLECTION OF YOUR INNER WORLD. THE HEATHER PROVIDES AN ENTHUSIASTIC PASSIONATE ENERGY, WITH NEVER A GAP BETWEEN THOUGHT, SPEECH AND ACTION. THIS REFLECTS A LOYALTY TO ONE'S TRUE SELF AND IS THE KEY TO THE HEATHER ENERGY.

THE BACH FLOWER REMEDY IS USEFUL WHEN PEOPLE HAVE BECOME SO PREOCCUPIED WITH THEMSELVES THEY HAVE NO THOUGHTS OR TIME TO GIVE TO OTHERS. THE HEATHER WILL HELP THEM FIND A GENEROSITY OF SPIRIT WHICH WILL HELP THEM TO BE AWARE OF OTHER PEOPLE'S PROBLEMS AND NEEDS. HEALING OURSELVES IS THE PLACE OF DEPARTURE FOR SEEING WHERE WE CAN HELP IN THE HEALING OF OTHERS. PEACE WITHIN YOURSELF MEANS YOU ARE OPEN TO GUIDANCE FROM within which will lead you to do what is right without any ulterior thought of reward and personal advantage.

A walk on a heather clad moor will lift the spirits and bring a calming soothing effect. The heather inspires us to go about our lives with this same lightness of spirit, which we can then pass on to others.

Healing is enhanced by a calm and peaceful state of mind. Heather will facilitate healing in conjunction with any other chosen method. Healing is an on-going process which depends on your every day life being as free from stress as possible. Use the enthusiastic energy of the heather to search out any areas of your life which are causing you stress, and find inspired ways to reduce this stress.

Communicating with Heather

Finding heather clad moors may not be easy. It might necessitate a trip or a holiday, which in turn might be just what you need to create space to look at your life.

Cutting some heather for your 18th Ogham stick, will mean you have a bundle of heather which you can bring home with you. Make this into bunches and give them to your friends — a sprig of lucky heather immediately lifts the spirit on sight.

The heather will bring joy and a passionate zest for life. It is a vowel stick in the Ogham so make combination letters with other sticks. Look at where the flow of energy between spirit and matter is flowing freely and which of the concepts and teachings you are not so comfortable with, and must work on. Combine with each of the other sticks in turn. Record your responses.

19 ASPEN
E·EADHADH

LISTEN TO YOUR INNER VOICE

THE SUPPORT OF LOVE

TRUST

LINKING TO THE SOURCE

UNDERLYING ENERGY

The Aspen is commonly referred to as the whispering tree, the talking tree, or the trembling tree. The Aspen's leaves quiver and whisper in the wind, lifting up their white underside and giving us the chance to hear what it has to tell us. Throughout the world, in many religions and cultures, the wind is associated with the voice of spirit. The Aspen teaches us the need to listen to our own inner voice, the voice of our own spirit, and any messages we might perceive. But our inner voice might not bring us clear messages. The messages born of fearful imaginings are not worth acting upon. So it is important that you trust yourself and your state of mind, this is the key to the Aspen energy. A state of peace, fearlessness and security arrived at through a realization that everything we do, and everything that happens to us is supported by a loving spirit is the still calm point from which we can trust our inner voice and our actions. There is nothing to fear but fear itself.

Dr. Bach wrote 'Once we come to realise that everything we do is supported by love, we are beyond pain and suffering, beyond care or worry or fear, beyond everything except the joy of life, the joy of death, and the joy of our own immortality....... We can walk that path through any danger, through any difficulty unafraid.'

The Aspen helps us overcome fear and anxiety and helps us find our inner reserves and strength from within. It grows by sending up new suckers which can become new trees. Thus an Aspen tree will generate hundreds of interconnecting trees all joined together at the roots, providing us with a clear image of continuity, growth and connection to the source.

Linking to the spiritual source, love, is the culmination of a spiritual journey. Everything leads to here and everything follows from here.

Communicating with Aspen

When linking to the Aspen with your 19th Ogham stick, be aware of the interlinking nature of this tree. Link the aspect of fearlessness to all the other trees and see which areas you still need to work on.

DEATH AND REBIRTH
NEVER-ENDING CYCLE
TRANSFORMATION
ACCESS TO THE ANCESTORS
ACCESS TO THE SPIRIT REALMS

UNDERLYING ENERGY

The Yew is the last tree of the tree Ogham. The end of the cycle. The wheel turns and the cycle begins again. The Yew teaches us about rebirth and transformation.

The Yew is often found in churchyards and ancient burial places. Many of the ancient yews in Britain's churchyards were there long before the churches were built on the sacred sites of the old religion. A new system of dating the yews estimates that some of these yews have been growing for 4,000 years! The Yew grows in a unique way. The branches grow down to form new stems which become the trunks of new trees still linked to the original tree. Also a new trunk can grow from the decaying mass of the old trunk. This is the power of rebirth and transformation which the Yew has to show us.

Death is fraught with a sense of loss, but the Yew teaches us to see it as part of a cycle of life. By turning to face our own death, through circumstances or as part of a growth exercise, we can come to the understanding that Universal Love is there supporting us through the transition of death, just as it is supporting us through the transition of life. Everything is interconnected.

The Yew has always been revered for providing a direct link to the ancestors and the spirit realms. Here there are angels, guides and guardians assigned to each one of us, whose purpose is to help us if we are open to their assistance.

The Yew reminds us there are other levels of existence beyond the one we see. By understanding the illusionary nature of our lives, we can consciously feel our connection to the wisdom which is always there, what was, what is, and what will be, always, continuously flowing, merging, transforming...... Life.

Communicating with Yew

The Yew will assist you in making journeys into the spirit realms. It can help you to make contact with your ancestors or guides who are always with you, offering their love and support. Trusting our intuition to act upon the messages we receive, will help us to make real progress in our inner healing, as the wheel turns and the death of one situation becomes the rebirth of another.

If you can, go and visit some of the really ancient Yews. These are nearly all in churchyards. Sometimes a group of Yews can be found in a wood. It is better perhaps to ask one of these for your 20th and last Ogham stick.

Use your Ogham stick for deep healing meditations, and inner travel into the astral plane.

It is thought that Ogham messages may have been written on Yew wood staves. Try writing a combination of Ogham fews which have a deep meaning for you. Use these combinations to create a unique vibration of inner understanding which can be used for talismans and healing wands.

USING YOUR OGHAM STICKS FOR DIVINATION

Divination is a method of learning things which would otherwise be hidden from us. It is a chance for our otherworld guides and helpers to communicate with us through an encoded system which can be interpreted and intuitively understood.

By building a system with the conscious mind, (in this case based on trees) a bridge is built between the conscious mind and the unconscious, which provides an open channel for a dialogue between these two aspects of ourselves. By making and using ogham sticks you are balanced in an act of sacred communication between the material world, and the world of spirit.

By building up your understanding of the different qualities of the trees, you can use this system of symbolic language to help you see the present moment in its fullest context, so that you can make clear decisions based on this overview.

There are no right or wrong ways of using the ogham sticks. Devise a method which feels right for you. The only thing which is important is that the stick(s) must be chosen intuitively and at random, not with the conscious mind.

You might throw the sticks in the air and see which land on top, or which sticks break away from the main group. These can then be interpreted in a creative and intuitive way.

The simplest method is to dip your hand into your bag of ogham sticks and pull one out. This will encapsulate the present moment, and guide your actions through your understanding of that tree.

You might ask for general guidance, or you might spend some time focused on a particular problem before you choose your stick.

A deeper reading is obtained by choosing three sticks at random from your bag. The sticks are laid out as follows:-

```
( 3rd Choice )
( 2nd Choice )
( 1st Choice )
```

The first choice (bottom stick) represents the underworld aspect. It will tell you what the root of the situation is. It also represents things hidden, or in the past.

The second choice (middle stick) represents the material world. It is the present moment caught in time. Interpret it in the light of the first few. It also represents your manifested power, your physical, mental, emotional and spiritual situation at this point in time.

The third choice (top stick) is the most fluid. It reflects the otherworld aspect. This is a realm where all possibilities exist, a series of parallel universes. This few will provide you with further insights into possible directions you are flowing towards. Understanding the underlying spiritual energy of this few will guide your actions towards the most positive outcome.

There is a need when interpreting the Ogham sticks, to fully trust your immediate impressions and insights. Don't worry about what your conscious mind thinks. Give your intuition a chance to guide your thoughts.

When you have completed your divination, write down the Ogham fews, with the date, and your immediate impressions. You could keep a special note book for this purpose.

For my children — Jerry, Jack & May.

My special thanks to my partner, Brian Boothby, for the words of Tomorrows Ancestor (Ash Tree illustration) and his loving support, which made writing this book possible.

I am also indebted to the trees for their wisdom and abundant gifts to the human race. My deepest wish is that humankind will come together to help save the trees: so many are dying, along with our polluted earth.

I also thank Buster Nolan, for his courage in speaking the truth about the trees' plight, and for his inspiring booklet 'Hello Human Relatives'.

It is important to remember that the interpretations I offer here are not fixed, and as your relationships with the trees' energies deepens, you will find your own unique understandings.

My particular interpretation of the Tree Ogham is centered around spiritual growth and healing. Steve Blamires in his book Celtic Tree Mysteries interprets it for magical use and details the medieval manuscripts. Edred Thorsson in The Book of Ogham suggests methods of casting for divination. Both books offer further doorways into understanding Celtic Tradition.

My thanks to Courtney Davis, for his inspiring interpretations of Celtic Art.

MAY LOVE GUIDE ALL OUR ACTIONS